Kingdom Leadership

LESSONS FOR YOUTH

by

David Burrows

Kingdom Leadership

Lessons for Youth

ISBN- 978-1-562297-70-1

Acknowledgements

First and foremost I must acknowledge my God, Jehovah and my Lord and Savior Jesus The Christ. I owe my present status as a globally recognized leader and specialist in Youth and Family Development to my conversion and my Faith. Before my conversion I was on a road to destruction but my life has been changed dramatically for the better because of this decision.

I must also acknowledge my wife Angela who is my closest friend on this earth and who has walked with me every step of my journey with love, faithfulness and assurance. My children who have made me extremely proud as a father, Arri who has been a leader from his youth and continues to lead in the financial and investment world. Davrielle who has followed me as an author, minister and leader even at a very young age.

My spiritual leaders and mentors, Dr. Myles Munroe, and Dr. Robyn Gool who have provided invaluable insight and example for me to follow.

To my friends in ministry locally and internationally, Dr. Richard Pinder, Pastor Henry Francis, Pastor Jay Mulllings and other leaders in the Bahamas Faith Ministries Fellowship. Pastor Mark Graham, Dr. Chris Hill, Pastor Mark Lawrence, Minister Kevin Harris, Minister Eric Fox, Rev. Clinton Minnis, Rev. Diana Francis, Apostle Carlos Reid, Pastor Chris Green and others around the world. My ITWLA family who are too many to mention.

My team at One Rib Publications especially Davrielle Burrows, my editor and my team of graphic artists.

Dedication

This is book is dedicated to my past and future spiritual sons and daughters and the next generation of leaders who will emerge.

Introduction

It has often been said that the greatest need in the world today is not money, resources or technology. The greatest need is leadership. Every country in the world has enough resources to support its population but the resources are often not distributed or utilized equitably or effectively because of defective, corrupt or inept leadership. The real problem is a lack of successful leadership. If we had leaders who are wise, accountable and subject to a higher authority then we would have good, Godly governance and the Bible states that when this type of government exists the people rejoice.

Unfortunately the leadership we are looking for may have to come from another generation as this current generation has squandered many opportunities to lead and govern effectively. The best way to get new leadership is to develop emerging leaders who are still young and can still be guided and directed on the right path. This book is about providing the next generation with simple tools they can use to develop their leadership potential. This is only a beginning as there will be further volumes in this series. Whether you are young or old please read, observe and put these lessons into practice. These are the lessons I have used to lead effectively in my sphere of influence and that others have also used for the same purpose.

Qualified to Speak?

I would not want to write a book about leadership if I had not become a leader myself. I do not claim to be the greatest or even the most famous leader but I believe my biography which ensues amply proves that I have qualified myself as a leader in both theory and practice. You are considered a leader when, without prodding or cajoling, others recognize you as a leader and willingly follow in your footsteps. It is on this basis that I submit to you my leadership credentials before I speak to you about leadership.

I did not start out as a leader, at least not in a positive sense but I believe my life is a testament of how a life can be transformed from negative to positive, from destruction to construction from the domain of darkness to the domain of light or as one would say, the Kingdom of Light. Initially I roamed the streets of Nassau, Bahamas as a troubled teen, introduced to drugs at the age of twelve, becoming a street drug dealer at the age of thirteen, forming a school gang at the age of fourteen, being suspended from school for assaulting a teacher at fourteen, thrown out of my own house for assaulting my father at fifteen years old. I found myself robbing students and others at the age of fifteen, committing shoplifting, burglary and other crimes at the age of sixteen, leading the police on a high speed chase at the age of seventeen and being arrested for possession of drugs. While in College I was arrested for burglary and handgun possession at the age of eighteen and finally I was placed on probation by the Sheriffs department and Dean of the first college I attended. This did not seem like the life of a future leader with worldwide influence in my arena but this is how my journey began.

During my second year of college I was influenced by a young man a few years older than me who had begun his own leadership journey and his leadership influence led me to a decision to dedicate my life to living a new lifestyle under a new "Lord" which transformed me into what I would eventually become. Pastor Robyn Gool was my first positive mentor who I allowed into my life. He helped to shape me into the man and leader I would become. As I grew and developed as a leader I was introduced to another mentor who further shaped my development as a leader and whose footsteps I followed in as he ascended to world leadership status, Dr. Myles Munroe. These two men helped me directly and indirectly to become a leader who others could follow and learn from and who would cause others to repeat the cycle as transformers and agents of positive change.

Consider these transformational leadership activities that qualifies Dr. Burrows to speak on this issue (Derived from the Biography of Dr. Dave Burrows):

- Upon graduation from College he decided on his own to assist friends he left behind from the streets who were on drugs or had life challenges and developed a drug rehabilitation and rescue program.
- He was hired by the Bahamas Governments' Ministry of Youth, Sports and Community Affairs where he established a number of programs directed at youth development such as Operation Experience (designed to give teens on the job experience in their teen years) and the Small Business Center.
- He started five businesses from scratch including , Speedy Lawn Service, King David's Fashions, One Rib Publications, Megabyte Computers, The Winners Touch and Tech TC, three of which are currently still active.
- He has become one of the foremost authorities in the world on Youth development and Youth Ministry.

- He is a lifetime Youth Ministry specialist with over 25 years of experience in youth development, training and mentoring.
- He pioneered many successful programs for youth affecting gangs including the “Peace on the Streets”, campaign with Carlos Reid and Youth Against Violence which saw over 1,000 gang members make commitments to Christ, many of whom went on to reform their lives and become productive citizens.
- He served as a consultant for churches, schools and youth leaders around the world (Africa, Europe, Canada, Caribbean, United States) and churches, pastors and entire organizations and denominations.
- Conducted Youth Ministry Training Events for Churches, Schools and Organizations worldwide
- Hosted Youth Alive youth conference attracting 5,000 teens each year in the month of July for 20 years
- Served as an advisor to the Bahamas Government and Cabinet on Youth matters advising the Bahamas Government as Chairman of the National Youth Advisory Council on three occasions.
- Founded and serves as President of Dave Burrows Youth and Family Ministries,
- Founder of Youth Alive Ministries.
- Founder and president of The Christian Youth Leaders Network and the Global Youth Ministry Leadership Network.
- President and founder of The Winners Touch, a motivational and business entity.

- Founder and CEO of Megabyte Computers a diversified computer company in Nassau, Bahamas.
- Founder and CEO of One Rib Publications a globally oriented publishing service.
- Has authored and published 12 books, including Making the Most of Youth Teenage Years, Sex and Dating, Kingdom Parenting which he co-authored with Dr. Myles Munroe and the Power of Positive Choices.
- Served as executive producer of six movies and three music soundtracks.
- Has appeared on many local and international television programs and events hosted by TBN, TD Jakes Potters Touch, Oral Roberts University, Messiah College, Armstrong Williams, The Potters House Denver, Dr. Fred Price and many others.
- Has spoken and conducted seminars extensively in the United States, Caribbean, Canada, Europe and Africa.
- Served as a business and technology consultant for many organizations.
- Clients have included corporations, civic and social organizations and churches.
- He is a longtime associate of Dr. Myles Munroe having served for many years as Vice President of both Bahamas Faith Ministries and Myles Munroe International.
- Has mentored and coached many individuals to personal and business success and continues to serve as both an inspirational and motivational speaker and life coach.
- Founded the Youth and Family Center a center for transformational strategies impacting, teens, young

adults and families through counselling, life coaching and mentoring.

- Member of the International Third World Leaders Association serving as Youth Ministry and Youth Development specialist.
- Served on the Bahamas National Drug Council for many years.

The five Questions Every Leader Must Answer

Where Does Leadership Begin?

Leadership always begins as an individual pursuit. If you cannot lead yourself you cannot lead others. You cannot lead yourself without self-discovery, self-actualization and self-governance. Dr. Myles Munroe stated that the first thing a leader must do is answer the five questions of the human soul. The answer to these questions form your philosophy from which your life emanates. Unanswered these question will lead to a life of futility and misunderstanding. The answer to these questions is the beginning of the leadership journey. What are these 5 questions?

1. Who am I? – This is the question of identity. If you do not know who you are you will take on the identity of others and will need others in order to feel validated. You are an original creation of God. There is only one of you.

2. Where am I from? – This is not about your location, ethnic background, nor your country of origin. You are not from your country, you are originally from heaven and you came from God via your parents. This is a question of heritage. If you came from God, regardless of whatever vehicle was

used there is a reason and purpose for your existence. If you came by accident there is no original purpose.

3. Why am I here? – You were not born to live in a cage. You are here for a reason that emanates from your "maker", "designer", or "manufacturer." There is meaning to your life, you are not an accident and you have a reason for your life. Knowing why you exist prevents you from doing things that are harmful to your existence. Finding your purpose is the key to life.

4. What can I do? - What is my potential? What abilities are built into me by my Creator? If you discover your gifts, talents abilities and potential you are equipped to live a full life because your potential causes you to continually develop until your maximize your gift. Your gift "makes room" for you.

5. Where am I going? - A question of destiny. If you've answered the first four questions then you should know that you are supposed to be going somewhere. You have a destination. Your destination is what keeps you alive.

Leadership Lesson #1 – Leaders Put The Kingdom First

Education is important, achievement is important, career is important and all these things are laudable. Education has its place, fame has its place, achievement has its place but for a young person to truly be successful you must be successful as a citizen and representative of your Kingdom. According to the Bible we belong to a Kingdom that exists on earth but is not based on earth. Our Kingdom is not a physical kingdom but one that extends to earth from God. Jesus prayed "thy Kingdom come, thy will be done" which implies that a Kingdom from another place (heaven) is supposed to be superimposed on earth or come to earth through representatives of that kingdom. The Kingdom of God is not age restricted so young people are supposed to be leaders on earth in their environment as representatives of this Kingdom. The Bible puts it this way, "2 Corinthians 5:18 All this is from God, who reconciled us to himself through Christ and gave us the ministry of reconciliation....vs [20] We are therefore Christ's ambassadors, as though God were making his appeal through us". The implication here is that we are leaders who represent the laws and mores of another Kingdom while we are here on earth. As a young person you are designated as a Kingdom ambassador and a designated leader on earth. Be first and foremost a "Kingdom" leader which means being in good standing with the King and qualified to be a representative. This means you have to know the laws, rules and benefits of your Kingdom in order to explain them to your friends and contacts. *A Kingdom leader causes God's Kingdom to be realized in whatever environment they are in.*

A young lady came to me who had been involved in our youth ministry for years and she had gone off to college. Most young people when they go to college will adopt the customs and mores of college life which in many cases will mean a departure from their "Christian" or "Kingdom" upbringing, where they end up engaging in promiscuous behavior or abusing drugs or alcohol. This young lady went into this environment and rather than conforming she acted as an ambassador, started a Bible study and mentoring group and caused other students who were wavering and struggling with the challenges of college life to be strengthened and return to the standards they observed in their early life.

One of the questions you must ask yourself is, "What are you doing as a Kingdom youth leader to cause the Kingdom to come in your environment?" If you are not influencing those around you to observe Godly principles and standards then you are not yet a leader or an ambassador. You must be a Kingdom leader.

Leadership Lesson #2 – Leaders Position Themselves for Influence and Success

One of the keys to leadership success as a young person is positioning. Growing up, I did not have the right attitude about leadership and became a "back bencher", someone who always sat at the back of the room, someone who never tried to be in front or serve in any leadership capacity. I used to have the wrong attitude about leadership. I remember when I was younger, I would never assume any position of leadership, if someone asked me to be a prefect (student leader) in school it was considered an insult because in my mind only soft people would be prefects. In every classroom I entered I immediately went to the back. In my mind nerds sat in front. Gangsters never sat in front according to my friends. Not only would I sit in the back, I would also make it a point to disturb other students and intimidate my teachers. This caused me to end up in detention, being expelled from school and have grades well below my potential, but in my mind I was “cool”.

If we fast forward a few years you will find that I became a Kingdom Citizen (Christian) but because of my upbringing and background I continued to sit in the back of the class. I was now a college student but my past beliefs caused me to be out of position. Through the help of mentors and the encouragement of teachers I changed position and moved to the front of the class. The impact on my studies and life was dramatic. I became more engaged and began to emerge as a leader. Leaders normally are people who are out front. Leaders end up at the top. If you want to be a leader, position yourself for leadership and success by always positioning yourself in front. If you are a prefect, a student president, chaplain, or RA you are in a position of influence and you can change your life and the lives of others through your position. Position yourself for success. The back is normally crowded with people who are lazy, unproductive, disruptive or afraid. Move to the front.

I grew up with an outlaw mentality and this caused me to miss many opportunities. Once I found my way I abandoned the street philosophy of underachievement. My change came through recognition, revelation and self-acceptance (God’s acceptance). I broke out from that mental prison and a kingdom leader was born. I became the influencer and not the influenced. I became God led, not friend led or media led; I was now led and influenced by Kingdom issues and pursuits.

Leadership Lesson #3 – Leaders Consult God when Making Plans

In this scripture God reveals what happens when young people make plans without consulting him.

ISA 30:1 "Woe to the obstinate children, "declares the LORD, "to those who carry out plans that are not mine, forming an alliance, but not by my Spirit, heaping sin upon sin; who go down to Egypt without consulting me; who look for help to Pharaoh's protection, to Egypt's shade for refuge. But Pharaoh's protection will be to your shame, Egypt's shade will bring you disgrace.

God expects us to consult Him before proceeding with our plans. This scripture says "Woe" which means watch out; there will be serious repercussions if you pursue the course of action you are currently pursuing. God is saying if you are choosing a girlfriend consult him first, if you are choosing a career consult him first, if you are choosing a college, or any major decision consult him first.

If you make plans without consulting God then you cannot blame him if your plans don't work out. For example a young lady came to me and said that she was serving God and wanted to be successful as a Christian but she had a boyfriend who smoked marijuana and did not like to come to church. Her plans in this case were plans that were made and an alliance formed without consulting God or His Spirit. Sadly she ended up pregnant with a baby that she had to raise on her own because the boyfriend left soon after the baby was born. The result would have been quite different if she had consulted God or one of His representatives before making plans and forming and unproductive alliance. Consulting God means becoming familiar with his principles and using them as the guiding point on which you make decisions, especially decisions about relationships.

Leadership Lesson #4 – Leaders are People of Resolve

DA 1:8 But Daniel resolved not to defile himself with the royal food and wine, and he asked the chief official for permission not to defile himself this way. Now God had caused the official to show favor and sympathy to Daniel, but the official told Daniel, "I am afraid of my lord the king, who has assigned because of you." Why should he see you looking worse than the other young men your age? The king would then have my head because of you. "Daniel then said to the guard whom the chief official had appointed "Please test your servants for ten days: Give us nothing but vegetables to eat and water to drink. Then compare our appearance with that of the young men who eat the royal food, and treat your servants in accordance with what you see." So he agreed to this and tested them

> for ten days at the end of the ten days they looked healthier and better nourished than any of the young men who ate the royal food. So the guard took away their choice food and the wine they were to drink and gave them vegetables instead. To these four young men God gave knowledge and understanding of all kinds of literature and learning. And Daniel could understand visions and dreams of all kinds. So they entered the king's service. In every matter of wisdom and understanding about which the king questioned them, he found them ten times better than all the magicians and enchanters in his whole kingdom.

Daniel was a young man who was given a choice to compromise and go with the flow or resolve to do what he knew to be right. He chose to do what was right even though it was difficult and unpopular. True leaders are not afraid to make unpopular decisions. True leaders have resolve in the face of opposition.

Leadership Lesson #5 – Leaders Understand the Value of Key Relationships

Your success as a leader is influenced by your relationships. Any persons you have a relationship with should add to your value. Leaders associate with people who increase their value and their mental, spiritual or emotional capacity. Some young people are in relationships that decrease their value and produce liabilities. Good leaders know the difference.

Here are some Key Relationships for Youth:

- Your relationship with God (The King) is the most important relationship in your life. You cannot function as an effective Leader without a proper relationship with the King. How can you represent (re – present) someone you do not know or have limited knowledge about. My relationship with God has influenced every aspect of my life. You need to know the King and what He requires of you. You have to study and know the commands of the King in order to represent Him. Each of us has 1,440 minutes in a day. How many minutes of your day are spent consulting with your King? God is not physically in our lives but we stay in touch with him by observing the principles written in the Bible and by praying, meditating, reading and listening to or viewing materials based upon His word and instructions.

- Another important relationship is family – When you represent the King you understand how he set things up. The first authority in life is your parents. They are not always right but they are of a higher rank than you. You have to respect the position even if you don't have respect for the person. All armies have ranks such as; recruit – private – corporal – sergeant – captain, commander in chief. A real leader has their relationships in proper order. In addition to your parents your siblings are in your life for a reason, you are placed in a family for a reason. Make sure that you maintain a good relationship with your family both vertically (parents) and horizontally (other siblings).

- Friends are another important relationship. It has been said, "Show me your friends and I will show you your future." The truth is, you will be just like your friends so you must have friends who are in line with the future you want. You are often closer to your friends than your family so you should make sure that you have friends who are going in the direction you want to go and who have a positive influence on your life. Remember friends should add value to your life. If you have a friend who does not increase your value you need new friends.

- Another key relationship is your relationship with a mentor or mentors. Mentors are older people who have been where you want to go and can advise you on the steps to get there. Successful leaders have mentors in their lives. In the Bible Timothy was mentored by the apostle Paul. In the movie titled "The Karate Kid" the Karate Kid was mentored by Mr. Miyagi who was older, more experienced and wiser. Seek out and stay attached to positive mentors if you want to be successful. Good leaders observe those who have gone before and incorporate the lessons learned into their lives.

Leadership Lesson #6 – Leaders Understand That Association Influences Destination

Who do you associate with? Do you associate with people or do people associate with you. Your friends represent your future. The people you hang around are a reflection of you. Do you have to fight to survive among your friends or is it easy to be with them? Do your friends share the same belief system? Do you attend the parties and see how much you can take without sinning? Are your close friends Christian or not? Are they wholesome? The Bible indicates that it is difficult for two persons to walk together if they are not in agreement? If you hang around with people who do not agree with your values you can find yourself in the enemies' bed. In the Bible, Sampson associated himself with Delilah because of her beauty, ignoring her values. She enticed him to leave his values and he ended up in the enemies' bed, losing his hair, his eyes and eventually losing his life.

Associate with people who share your values and who add value to your life. I recall as a young person my associates were gangsters, drug dealers, thugs and bad boys. What did I become? I became exactly like my friends. Eventually I was the one influencing others into evil; I had become a thug because I decided to hang around thug living. Years later and many revelations later I changed my associations and my future changed. My new friends were leaders, business persons, pastors and persons of positive influence. My future was impacted by the friends I associated with. I went from being on drugs and running from the police to becoming a husband, father, businessman, motivational and inspirational speaker, travelling the world, writing books and advising leaders of churches, governments and organizations. Remember your associations are vital to your destination. Associate with people who are where and what you want to become.

Leadership Lesson #7 – Leaders are Servants First

Service is essential. Every Kingdom requires service. Every Kingdom has duties. Determine to serve. Leaders begin with serving. Give back, give back to God, give back to your community, give back to your parents, and give back to your school through service. Service is a way of showing gratitude. Jesus said that service is the key to greatness and He proved it by serving. In the book of Luke the story is told about Jesus' response to the disciples' quest for greatness. 22:24 "also a dispute arose among them as to which of them was considered to be greatest. Jesus said to them, "The kings of the Gentiles lord it over them; and those who exercise authority over them call themselves Benefactors. But you are not to be like that. Instead, the greatest among you should be like the youngest, and the one who rules like the one who serves. For who is greater, the one who is at the table or the one who serves? Is it not the one who is at the table? But I am among you as one who serves."

Remember that your gifts talents and abilities are God's gift to you, what you do with them is your gift back to him. Whatever you have been given you should use to serve others and make their lives better. Jesus said the greatest should first become a servant. He said He came to serve. Don't pass up opportunities to serve. In the words of a song penned by friends of mine (Myles Munroe and the late Dr. Mark Bethel) "We were born to lead, to set the captives free, we will serve the Lord, so that every man might see, that the greatest way to lead is in serving God, Yes, I was born to lead".

Never wait until you are old to serve. The earlier you begin serving the greater your head start is to becoming a true leader.

Leadership Lesson #8 – Leaders Value Knowledge

Leaders are readers. Leaders are consumers of information. The Bible says people perish because of a lack of knowledge. True leaders are always asking questions. Why? Because your value increases according to the questions you receive answers too. If the question is, "How I can get my car started?" Then the mechanic who possesses that knowledge has an increased level of value. The more information you have, the more value. At 12 years of age Jesus sat with adults and asked questions. This was an example for us to follow. Jesus was the ultimate leader and as a youth He sat with adults and asked questions. If you want to be a leader, follow in His footsteps. Whatever you want to be in life find someone who is already there and ask questions. If you aspire to be a doctor, visit the hospital or the doctor's office and ask someone who is already a doctor to answer your questions. If you want to be a teacher, speak to the teachers in your school and ask them the questions you need to know to become a teacher. If you want to own a business in the future, talk to businessmen today who are successful and let them educate you on the process. Never stop learning. A good leader is a reader. The more you know the more valuable you are. If you want to succeed in court you must know your constitutional rights. If you know your rights and you have knowledge of your environment and you know and understand the times you can make wise decisions.

Remember that the more you learn in life the more you will earn. The more you read the more you will succeed. Spend your time learning and increasing your value. The programs you watch on television, the music you listen to, and the people you hang around should all increase your knowledge which will in turn increase your value. Make sure you read books on subjects that increase your knowledge and value. Over the years I have constantly read books, listened to CD's and watched videos that inspire me and give me information that I do not have.

Leadership Lesson #9 – Leaders Seek Wisdom

Knowledge is important but even more important than knowledge is wisdom. You can know something but not know what to do with it. Wisdom is knowing what to do with knowledge. Knowledge alone is not enough. Jesus encourages us to be "...Wise as serpents, yet harmless as doves." This means you must know what to do with your knowledge and how to operate in different environments. Wisdom is knowing when to do what. Daniel knew things others did not know because God gave him wisdom. Knowledge is vital but even more important than knowledge is wisdom. There are doctors who know that smoking a cigarette is detrimental to their health but they still smoke. They have knowledge but no wisdom. One of the most valuable entities of all is wisdom. The book of Proverbs indicates that wisdom is valued far above rubies and pearls. Too many people have knowledge but lack wisdom.

Leadership Lesson #10 – Leaders Understand the Necessity of Sacrifice

It is impossible to achieve anything great in life without sacrifice. Sacrificing means you give up something you would like to do to achieve something greater. An athlete sacrifices sleep, fun and idle time in order to achieve victory in their sport. They are willing to abuse their bodies, deny themselves certain foods, and forego parties and even time with their spouse in order to achieve a goal. Leadership means sacrifice. Followers are the ones who prefer not to sacrifice but leaders look at sacrifices as a necessary part of the road to success. What have you sacrificed? What are you willing to sacrifice in order to achieve your goals? A good education requires study time when you would prefer it to be party time. I remember speaking to one young member of our church who had become a collegiate athlete. She told me that she loved running but it took a toll on her body. She noted that to this day she endured pain, aches and stress because of constantly lifting weights and stressing her body in the past. This was the sacrifice and the price she had to pay to be a successful athlete. The Bible admonishes us to present our "bodies a living sacrifice", meaning we deny what our body wants because we have a higher goal. I spoke with another athlete who told me that in between Olympic races, she would sit it a tub of ice in order to reduce inflammation so she could run the next day. We see the glory but we don't know the story behind the glory. If you want to be a leader you must be willing to sacrifice to achieve your goal. Sacrifice for the good of the Kingdom but also for your own good. Give up some things to get some things. If you sacrifice in the background, going un-noticed, God will put you in the right place at the right time. Every great leader, great businessman, athlete, artist or entertainer has walked the road of sacrifice before they achieved fame and glory. Sacrifice is also necessary to maintain your success. If you stop sacrificing and think you have arrived this may be the beginning of your downfall.

Lesson #11 – Leaders Know How to Prioritize

Prioritizing means putting things into proper order based on importance. There are some things in life we can have but the question is, is it the right time to have them? There are some things we can do now but the question is how does it rank in terms of importance. A leader is one who knows how to prioritize. In life you will have any number of options and choices. If you want to be successful you will have to determine which option is a priority and which option can wait for another time. Your priorities are determined by what you want to achieve and the type of life you want to have. If you belong to God your priorities will be determined by what He says the priorities ought to be. What is most important now? God says your priorities should be:

1. Love Him.

2. Love and value yourself.

3. Love others.

4. Obey your parents.

5. Learn the lessons appropriate with your stage of life.

6. Get an education.

7. Pursue your purpose.

8. Maximize Your potential.

As a teenager some things are priority and other things are not. God wants you to have sex but He wants you to wait for the right time and under the conditions He designed it to function best. It is important to know what the priority according to God's plan is. Sex is important but there are some things that are a higher priority like education and socialization and finding your purpose. Learn to prioritize in life according to what is appropriate for this season of life. As a teenager now is not the season for a family so why have a committed love relationship when you are not equipped to handle it? Prioritize.

Lesson #12 – Leaders Understand Timing

When King David was a youth he prepared himself in obscurity for years before he became famous. He was prepared and because he had spent time in preparation at the right time God set things up for him to go into action. The preparation came first, then when the time was right he was selected to fulfill his purpose. Here is a sample of his story 1SA 16:7 But the LORD said to Samuel, "Do not consider his appearance or his height, for I have rejected him. The LORD does not look at the things man looks at. Man looks at the outward appearance, but the LORD looks at the heart." So he sent and had him (David) brought in. He was ruddy, with a fine appearance and handsome features. Then the LORD said, "Rise and anoint him; he is the one. "...A champion named Goliath, who was from Gath, came out of the Philistine camp. He was over nine feet tall. He had a bronze helmet on his head and wore a coat of scale armor of bronze weighing five thousand shekels; ...When Eliab, David's oldest brother, heard him speaking with the men, he burned with anger and asked, "Why have you come down here? And with whom did you leave those few sheep in the desert? I know how conceited you are you came down only to watch the battle."

"Now what have I done?" said David. "Can't I even speak?" He then turned to someone else and brought up the same matter, and the men answered him as before. What David said was overheard and reported to Saul, and Saul sent for him. David said to Saul, "Let no one lose heart on account of this Philistine; your servant will go and fight him."

(True young leaders do things they are not supposed to do yet)....Saul replied, "You are not able to go out against this Philistine and fight him; you are only a boy, and he has been a fighting man from his youth." ....Saul said to David, "Go, and the LORD be with you." (God Help You) Then Saul dressed David in his own tunic. He put a coat of armor on him and a bronze helmet on his head. David fastened on his sword over the tunic and tried walking around, because he was not used to them. " "I cannot go in these," he said to Saul, "because I am not used to them." Then he took his staff in his hand, chose five smooth stones from the stream, put them in the pouch of his shepherd's bag and, with his sling in his hand, approached the Philistine. Meanwhile, the Philistine, with his shield bearer in front of him, kept coming closer to David. He looked David over and saw that he was only a boy, ruddy and handsome, and he despised him. .... (David) Today I will give the carcasses of the Philistine army to the birds of the air and the beasts of the earth, and the whole world will know that there is a God in Israel. As the Philistine moved closer to attack him, David ran quickly toward the battle line to meet him. When the Philistines saw that their hero was dead, they turned and ran. Then the men of Israel and Judah surged forward with a shout and pursued the Philistines to the entrance of Gath and to the gates of Ekron. David took the Philistine's head and brought it to Jerusalem, and he put the Philistine's weapons in his own tent.

There is a time and place for everything. David prepared and when the appointed time came he was able to execute to perfection. This season may be a season of preparation for you for something big in your future. Wait until you complete this season before you enter the next season. Once you are prepared and the time is right you will rise to where you are supposed to be.

Lesson #13 – Leaders Create Their Own Legacy

You are only on this earth for a limited time. You were born for a purpose and designed to leave a mark in this world. Focus your attention on your legacy. It is good to celebrate stories of the past and to talk about the achievements of others but you need to create your own stories for others to hear about, read about and celebrate. There are books that you are supposed to write and books that are supposed to be written about you. Get started while you are young and don't wait for another time to begin. Do you want to be a real leader? Do you want to know some things others don't know? Do you want inside information? If so you must prepare and equip yourself to build your own legacy. You have to do what David did, what Joseph did, what Daniel did. They prepared themselves to lead and build a legacy that would last. What will people remember you for? What stand will you take, what deed will you do that will be remembered for generations? It begins with you recognizing that you have a purpose. There is a plan for your life and the plan is for you to be great. Find your area of greatness, develop your gifts, your talents and your abilities and build your legacy. I began my journey to legacy by simply being faithful and trying to help my friends. As I pursued my purpose others began to recognize the legacy I was building. Due to my diligence and obedience to "my" purpose I was able to establish a legacy of revolutionary change in the area of youth ministry and youth work.

Lesson #14 – Leaders Understand Humility "God gives grace to the humble..."

Humility is recognizing your worth, your value, your gifts, talents and abilities but never flaunting or taking credit for what you have been blessed with. The Bible tells us that pride and boasting are the predecessors to a fall but humility is the predecessor to elevation.

Proverbs 16:18-19 New King James Version (NKJV)

> [18] Pride goes before destruction, And a haughty spirit before a fall. [19] Better to be of a humble spirit with the lowly, than to divide the spoil with the proud.

How can you demonstrate humility? Learn to not get puffed up or arrogant when you achieve great things, say thank you and give glory to God. When you are criticized don't attack those who criticize you, simply say to them, "Thank you for your opinion." A humble person is not moved by either criticism or praise. They have an internal compass that responds to purpose. Let others speak about you and praise you, don't brag about yourself or your accomplishments. Just fulfill your purpose and your mission and in time God will elevate you to where you were designed to be.

Lesson #15 - Leaders Recognize the Characteristics of a Leader

When you are a leader you recognize what it takes to be a leader. A leader:

- Is someone who shows others the way. A leader often does not have a trail to follow; they create a trail that others follow. A new trail requires extra work because the path has never been cleared.

- Makes decisions and does not wait for others to make decisions for them. Leaders do not wait around to see who is going to make a decision. Leaders will assess the situation and respond accordingly by making a decision.

- A Prototype (not a stereotype) – The first of a thing. Followers look for something that is already established and seek to copy it. Leaders establish new things; they produce the first of a thing rather than copying what others have done.

- A Thinker – People who change the world change it through ideas. Leaders are thinkers who are constantly coming up with ideas to impact their world. The people who have changed the world have done so because they have spent their time thinking about solutions rather than complaining about problems.

- Leaders are drivers and not passengers – Passengers do not know the destination and they do not have control of the journey because they are not holding the wheel. Drivers know the destiny and control the steering wheel. They know where they are going and control their destiny and are in a position to make the right choices. They are also in a position to steer away from trouble.

If you want to be a leader you must recognize what characterizes leaders.

Lesson #16 – Leaders Answer the Leadership Questions

- Who do you need to make a decision? – Leaders don't need a crowd to make a decision.
- How many close friends do you have? – Leaders do not have many close friends because leaders tend to live like eagles rather than chickens. Chickens flock together and keep their eyes to the ground; eagles soar alone and keep their head to the sky.
- How many times have you done things others are not doing? – If you are only doing what others are doing then you are not a leader. Leaders do things that others are not doing. They create a path of their own while followers follow the path that has been created.
- Leaders take stands that others are unwilling to take. If you are not willing to be unpopular or to be ridiculed you will not be a leader. Leaders face unpopularity, ridicule and scorn but they are driven by an internal motivation.
- Whose approval do you need to proceed? – If you have to wait on others to approve you before you proceed, you are not a leader. Leaders do not seek the approval of many; they seek Gods approval and the approval of a small select group of their mentors.

Lesson #17 – Leaders Understand the Leadership Keys

Leaders are:

- Goal, Mission and Purpose Driven – not driven by opinions or popular culture
- Focused – on their goal – leaders learn to lock in on a goal and stay glued to that goal. Their focus prevents them from being distracted.
- Stable – Leaders are not easily swayed. Leaders form opinions and make decisions based upon facts as they see them. Leaders once convinced don't waver from their convictions. They can be depended upon because they don't flip flop or waiver.
- Playing to their strength – Leaders know their strong points and don't try to become something they are not equipped for. Great leaders recognize what their strengths are and focus in on their strengths.
- Knows how to follow (authority) – Good leaders learn to flow well before leading well. Do you know how to obey authority? This scripture shows us how to follow authority before we are elevated to positions of authority. He. 13:17 Obey your leaders and submit to their authority. They keep watch over you as men who must give an account. Obey them so that their work will be a joy, not a burden, for that would be of no advantage to you.

- Combine gifts to overcome deficiencies – Leaders recognize they don't have all the answers so they find others who possess strengths in areas where they are weak and they utilize the gifts of others in order to achieve goals that benefit all.

Lesson #18 – Leaders Think Differently

How a Leader Thinks

Leaders are solution oriented and not problem oriented. When a leader sees a problem they don't spend an inordinate amount of time complaining about the problem, they begin seeking a solution and concentrate their energies on the solution and not the problem.

Leaders are able to eliminate "noise". Noise is the voices around who will both criticize and praise. A basketball player learns to ignore the pomp pons and flags being waved when he is shooting a free throw. He ignores the noise and concentrates on the goal, eliminating the noise and distractions from his mind.

Leaders understand the difference between assets and liabilities. I always say, "I can be stupid all by myself; I don't need to hire five people to help me be stupid." If people enter my life they need to increase my value. A young lady came to me and explained that her boyfriend was a drug user and unemployed but he was a "nice" guy. I asked her if she was stupid by accident or intentionally stupid. I asked her why she would add liabilities to her life when she should be building assets. Everyone who enters your life should increase your value, which is what assets do. Liabilities decrease your value.

A leader thinks of solutions and value. Apple computers changed the computer, electronics and music world because they decided to "Think Differently."

Lesson #19 – Leaders Make Others Better

What happens to the people who come into your life? Do they leave you bitter or better? A leader makes others better. There are some people in life who want to gain and attain and achieve and accomplish but all of their focus is on themselves. Good leaders make others better. What happens to the people who hang around you or work and serve with you? If you are a good leader the people around you will continually become better. The greatest sports figures are the ones who make the whole team better. When I think of great basketball players there are several to choose from but two that stand out in my mind are Magic Johnson and LeBron James. Both men could easily rack up numerous individual goals but they chose to make their teammates better. They could both take over a game when necessary but they would often reward teammates by making an extra pass and giving up an opportunity that they have to ensure that their teammates were rewarded for hustle and dedication. Great leaders get others to maximize their potential even if they have to give up individual glory.

Lesson #20 - Leaders Never Fear Failure

One of the things that strikes fear into all of us is failure. Some people are so afraid of failing that they fail to try. Fear of failure can be paralyzing. Leaders do not have the option of fearing failure. Failure is a part of life and is often a precursor to success. The best basketball player in the world shoots 50% meaning he fails on one out of every two attempts. The best baseball player only succeeds one out of every three tries. They do not pay attention to the missed shots or the strikeouts, they focus on the hits. If you want to succeed never focus on the misses, live for the hits. You are remembered for what you overcome and not what you avoid. Everyone who has succeeded has had to overcome many failures but we never talk about their failures. We remember them for their one or two successes and not the failures. In life you only need one success to make your mark. Keep seeking success and ignoring failures. Thomas Edison who invented the light bulb did over 10,000 experiments before he achieved success. We never ask about his 10,000 failures we live off of his one success.

Leadership Lesson #21 - Leaders Value Mentorship

Leaders find someone who is or has been where they want to go. I had a conversation with a young lady the other day who wanted to become a doctor. I told her this is very noble and proceeded to ask her a very important question. I asked her if she visited or worked in the hospital yet and had she spoken with practicing physicians. She said to me that she had not done either except to visit a relative in the hospital. I told her that must change because the best way to get to the future you desire is to speak with and be mentored by someone who is already there. The best source of knowledge is someone who has achieved what you would like to achieve. This is one of the reasons that at twelve years old Jesus sat in the temple speaking with the elders and leaders. Luke 2:46 -47 [46] Now so it was that after three days they found Him in the temple, sitting in the midst of the teachers, both listening to them and asking them questions. [47] And all who heard Him were astonished at His understanding and answers. A mentor in your field can provide valuable information that can have a major impact on your future. History is filled with examples of mentors who have impacted the lives of others and produced great leaders. In the Bible Jesus mentored twelve disciples who then changed the world. The Apostle Paul mentored Timothy. Great leaders understand and value the role of mentors.

Leadership Lesson #22 – Leaders Are Not Intimidated by Man, Status or Position

Leaders respect all men but do not allow themselves to be intimidated by men regardless of their status or influence in life. Leaders realize that all men are created equal and each has unique gifts and qualities. None are placed on a higher plane or blessed with superhuman powers. With this being the case a leader respects men and their positions but never allows a position to become a source of intimidation. We must remember that all humans go to the bathroom, get dressed, eat and sleep alike. We are identified by our positions and accomplishments but these accomplishments do not give us a superior human status. In the story of David and Goliath, David respected the physical appearance and fighting ability of Goliath but he was not intimidated. This was an extraordinary feat because all of the great men of his day were clearly intimidated. The difference with David was that he was more confident in what was on the inside rather than what he saw on the outside. Leaders will often go where others fear to tread. Martin Luther King Jr., Nelson Mandela, Mahatma Ghandi all had reason to fear but they refused to be intimidated. People who change the world do not let men intimidate them.

Lesson #23 - Leaders Are Content But Not Complacent

A good leader is not overly obsessed with their goals or success. A leader aggressively and wholeheartedly pursues their goals but not at the expense of their morals, family or things they deem important. This may sound like a contradiction for a leader to be content but contentment does not mean a lack of drive or passion. A good leader is content with where they are but not complacent. They are always seeking new ideas and means of achieving but they learn to be content after they know they have done their best. Persons who do not understand contentment can end up committing suicide when they fail to reach a goal. Contentment comes when you know you have done your best and there will be another day or another opportunity to conqueror. Jesus said, "What does it profit a man if he gains the whole world and loses his soul". Leaders' value accomplishment but they are content when they have done their best. They don't become obsesses with achievement. Leaders keep things in perspective. Leaders learn to appreciate what they have accomplished, seek after their goals but not become obsessed with achievement. A leader is satisfied when they have done their best and unsatisfied if they have not done their best. I heard a story recently about a young lady who was an accountant, lawyer, and financier and achieved great heights in the business world. She committed suicide and everyone tried to figure out what happened, why did someone who had such a bright future take her own life. The answer was she was continually discontent no matter what she achieved. The new goal had to be achieved in a given time span and if not all the other accomplishments did not matter. What a sad way to live. Learn to be content when you have done your best.

Lesson #24 – Leaders Know How to Improvise

The people who lead and change the world often do not know what the solution to a problem is ahead of time so they have learned to improvise to solve problems. Improvising means coming up with a solution that is not written in a book or manual. In the movies we see examples of improvisation all the time. In many James Bond movies you would find that he is caught in a situation where there is seemingly no way out but rather than give up or be afraid, he thinks on the spur of the moment and comes up with a solution just in time to save him or a friend. When I was much younger there was a TV character called MacGyver who would find anything in a room or yard and come up with a tool that would solve his problem. These are fictional examples but they reflect the characteristic of creativity and improvisation. When you are in charge remember that everyone is looking to you to solve the problem. Leaders often create new answers to questions because they are forced to. A leader is always thinking of solutions and where there is no manual they come up with solutions that others will end up following. I can recall many occasions when I had to improvise to solve a problem. Leaders sometimes amaze themselves on the ideas they come up with. I heard a story that a builder had built a hotel and realized that due to growth there were not enough elevators and space to put elevators in his building.

Realizing the difficulty he faced he thought about it for a while and then came up with the idea to put the elevator on the outside of the building which then became a trend that many other builders subsequently used. A leader improvises to get the most out of the least resources.

Lesson #25 – Leaders Are Doers

Leaders do not sit on the sidelines they make the headlines. Leaders are not content with seeing the world change; they want to change the world. Followers are content to watch things go wrong and wait for someone else to fix it. Followers will sit by and complain even as things fall apart around them. A leader will see a problem and decide to become a part of the solution. A leader will see a problem in his city and decide to run for the office of mayor because he or she wants to be in a position to affect change. Leaders are creators. I heard a story about a young girl only fourteen years old who decided to change her life economically. In the midst of one of the worst recent recessions when people were complaining about property values going down and others were becoming depressed she saw an opportunity and took advantage of it. She sold small items to her friends as a small business and accumulated several thousand dollars. She then borrowed a few thousand dollars from her mother and purchased a depressed home for $15,000.00. She then put the home on rent for $700.00 per month and became a home owner and landlord at fourteen years old. The rental income on her property will be at least $8,400 a year for the rest of her life. In ten years she would have earned at least $80,000. This is an example of a doer.

Leadership Lesson #26 - Leaders Discover and Develop Their Gifts

Your gifts will make room for you. Your gifts elevate you and create opportunities. Leaders recognize the value of gifts and develop them. Every human is born with unique gifts. Some are obvious while others are subtle. Many people go through life possessing tremendous gifts that they never develop. Your gifts revolve around what you are uniquely equipped to do. A bird is born with the gift of flight. A fish is born with swim. These are obvious gifts. Other gifts are not so obvious. A good or great leader will look within and discover their unique gifts, develop them and use them as stepping stones to a bright future. Maybe you have an athletic talent or a gift in the area of hospitality or communication. Whatever your gifts are leaders never allow gifts to go undiscovered or go to waste, they discover their gifts, develop them and use these gifts to elevate their lives and the lives of others. What is your gift? Perhaps you are good with business. Perhaps you are good with technology. If you discover your gift don't leave it dormant or wait for others to pull it out of you. Develop your gift and use it to advance your life and the lives of others.

Lesson #27 - Leaders Know the Importance of a Plan

Leaders are planners. Success begins with effective planning. In the building industry every prospective home builder has to submit a building plan that indicates where every item in the house will be such as bedrooms, bathrooms, kitchen, light switches, toilets before the builder is allowed to begin building. In the same way leaders have plans for their lives at every stage. As a leader you should have a plan for your life that indicates what you will be doing every step of the way. Plans can always be revised but you should always begin with a plan. Every business should begin with a business plan. Planning is essential to success in every arena of life. If someone asks the question what will you be doing five years from now it should be easy to answer because you should have it already planned. Perhaps your plan is to be in college, perhaps your plan is to start a business, perhaps your plan is to take a year off to travel the world and explore. Whatever your plans are they should be written down and. Most people who fail do so because they never had a plan for success. Leaders always have a plan. A leader is a "Man with a Plan". Plans can be adjusted or modified but where there is no plan there is no map of destiny. Plans show us the end so we can go back to the beginning and walk it out. Prepare now (for tomorrow).

Lesson #28 – Leaders Never Give Up

Life can be challenging no matter what your age. It is easy to give up when things seem hard, if you are disappointed or if you fail to achieve your goal in the first instance. Leaders do not give up easily because they are goal driven and see the big picture. The road to success is often long and hard and filled with challenges, traps, disappointment, enemies and setbacks. Ordinary people give up when they are faced with specter of defeat. Leaders are not. Leaders press through the most difficult circumstances and stay focused on the goal when others would have given up. Last year I saw a story on CNN that demonstrated the 'never give up' spirit. A young lady was homeless and faced extreme circumstances yet she ended up being the valedictorian of her class. If anyone had an opportunity to give up it was this young lady. Can you imagine waking up every day and you do not have a permanent place to live. You have to live in shelters, sleep under different roofs from week to week, unsure of where the next meal was coming from. A situation like this can be disheartening but she chose not to allow her circumstances to defeat her, she never gave up. I understand that when her story was seen on CNN she no longer had to worry about schooling because she was offered housing and a scholarship to College. When you refuse to give up others recognize you and assist you. Leaders love to see others who have chosen to overcome rather than quit.

Lesson #29 - Leaders Are Self-Controlled

The hardest discipline is self-discipline. It is easy for us to follow rules that are given by parents or authorities. The hard part is when you have to discipline yourself. Great leaders are first masters of themselves, their habits, their desires and their distractions. If you are able to control yourself it is easier to lead because you can require that others exercise self-control, because you have. We are often defeated in life by the things within our control that we fail to control. Failure to control food intake can result in obesity. Failure to control sex drive can result in premature pregnancy, sexually transmitted diseases, betrayal, disappointment and broken relationships. The Bible admonishes us to Tit. 2:6 Similarly, encourage the young men to be self-controlled. In everything set them an example by doing what is good. In your teaching show integrity, seriousness and soundness of speech that cannot be condemned, so that those who oppose you may be ashamed because they have nothing bad to say about us. God values self-control and expects it, especially of those who lead.

Lesson #30 - Leaders Are Self-Confident

Leaders have discovered their gifts and recognize their potential and are ready to pursue their purpose and destiny. Leaders believe in their abilities and potential. Leaders are confident to the point that others opinions of their value is irrelevant. Leaders experience a level of comfort in themselves that causes them to dismiss doubts and fears and remain established and convinced of their value. Self-confidence comes from research, preparation, practice and experience. The more you learn about God, yourself, your abilities and your gifts and the more you take the step of exposing yourself to the world through accepting challenges, the more self-confident you become. You become supremely confident when you have succeeded at doing something similar to what you plan to do. You are self-confident when you know your ability and you know your God's ability to deliver. A basketball player is confident when he steps to the line to make a free throw because he has developed his skill, practiced and experienced success many times before. In life you must prepare yourself mentally, physically and emotionally and allow yourself to be tested through experiences then you become self-confident. Self confidence in one area can translate to other areas because you know what you have already accomplished and you are not afraid because you know what you have already accomplished previously. Self-confidence allows you to take a leadership role.

Lesson #31 – Leaders Are Proud But Not Arrogant

There are people in the world who are proud to the extent that they are obnoxious. Great leaders have pride but are not belligerent and arrogant about it. Jesus provided the prime example. He was extremely proud yet incredibly humble. He never thought too highly of himself to visit people of lower estate. He was proud but not arrogant, extremely confident but yet extremely humble. He entertained children, he spoke with widows, and he met with tax collectors and "sinners". Leaders who are arrogant forget where they came from and start to believe their own hype. Arrogant individuals tend to attribute their success and their accomplishments to their own efforts and forget to be thankful and humble. Proud people revel in their success but learn not to focus the attention on themselves. They acknowledge those who have helped them get where they are and share the glory. An arrogant person will spend the entire press conference focusing on themselves and reminding people of how great they are. Arrogant people maintain an air of superiority and look down on others. Take pride in who you are but never look down on others or try to diminish others in order to elevate yourself.

Lesson #32 - Leaders Have Firm Convictions

Leaders study and evaluate life and make their decisions based upon a set of core beliefs that govern their lives. They study life and become convinced of what is right and wrong and translate those beliefs into a value system that serves as the basis for their actions. Leaders recognize that thoughts become precepts; precepts becomes ideas, ideas become concepts, concepts become convictions, convictions become beliefs, beliefs becomes ideologies, Ideologies becomes philosophies and philosophy becomes lifestyle. Convictions form the basis for your actions and ultimately your lifestyle. Good leaders are convinced of their beliefs and are driven to act on their convictions. Great leaders are remembered for their stand on their convictions. In the Bible Joseph, who was known as the prince of Egypt, chose to stand by his convictions and not sleep with the Pharaoh's wife even though she constantly harassed him. He had strong convictions to the point where he ran as she was tearing his clothes off. Nelson Mandela, Dr. Martin Luther King Jr., Mahatma Gandhi, were all great leaders who stood on their convictions no matter how unpopular they became or no matter what threats they received, even to their own lives. What are your convictions? What are you willing to stand on in the face of opposition and bribes? A young lady who has convictions will refuse to sleep with a man no matter how much money he has or how popular he is. The dictionary definition for conviction is, "a fixed or firm belief". When you have convictions you are not easily swayed by public opinion, pressure or bribe.

Lesson #33 – Leaders Have Personal Vision

Leaders see what followers don't. Joel. 2:28 states, "And afterwards, I will pour out my Spirit on all people. Your sons and daughters will prophesy, your old men will dream dreams, your young men will see visions. 2:29 Even on my servants, both men and women, I will pour out my Spirit in those days. This scripture shows us God's thoughts about vision. The people who change the world are people who see things others don't see even if they are all looking at the same thing. Steve Jobs and the great scientists of his day all looked at the same thing but he saw something they didn't see. At 18 years old he saw something called a "personal computer", a device that up until that time never existed. He took his vision and created what came to be known as Apple computers and changed the world. His motto for Apple Computers was "Think Differently". He realized that he did not get where he ended up by thinking like everyone else. Leaders tend to think different even when they see the same thing that everyone else sees. Vision is different from sight. When you have vision you see things even when your eyes are closed. When you have vision you see a decade when others are seeing the next day. An eagle is able to see the smallest object up to four miles away. A chicken sees only a few yards away.

Lesson #34 – Leaders Understand Purpose and Pursue It

What is purpose? Dr. Myles Munroe explained purpose in his book "The Pursuit of Purpose" this way. He noted that the purpose of a thing is the intent in the mind of the creator or maker of a thing. What is the purpose of a car? – Transportation of persons or cargo from one point to another. What is the purpose of a house? – A dwelling place for a group of people to provide shelter them and protect them from the elements. What is the purpose of an airplane? – To transport persons from one point to another over terrain and territories that cannot be traversed by a car, train or boat. What is the purpose of a man? – This is the hard question. The answer lies in who made man. If there is no maker there is no purpose. If we evolved we do not have a reason for what we do. Man's purpose comes from the design in the mind of his creator. What is the purpose of a woman? What is the purpose of a family? Purpose is the key to life. Without purpose life has no meaning. Dr. Munroe further explained that wherever purpose is not known abuse is inevitable. Purpose gives birth to hope and instills passion to act. You lose your edge when you lose your way (lose sight of your purpose).Proverbs 29:18 states, "Where there is no revelation,[a] the people cast off restraint; but happy is he who keeps the law". A leader must find their personal purpose and reason for existence and pursue that purpose as a lifelong goal. You will never really be fulfilled until you find and pursue your purpose.

Lesson #35 - Leaders Are Faithful in Small Things

No one gets promoted on a job if they have not proven themselves faithful on their initial assignments. You are promoted if you are faithful in the little assignment before you get the big assignment. How can you trust someone who has never completed a small task? Jesus gave the example in the Bible of three men who were given talents (responsibilities). The one who was given the smallest or least talent hid it while the ones who were given more invested and reproduced. When the judge came back to review their progress he rewarded the ones who were faithful to their assignment but he punished the one who was unfaithful. As a leader you will never become what you were designed to be if you are not faithful in the small things. The best leaders are leaders who began by cleaning the bathroom or driving the bus. They have learned to be faithful in small things among people others consider insignificant and as they grew and developed they could be trusted with more important tasks. Be faithful in small things and watch promotion come to your life. There is a reason for graduations in school. They signify your faithfulness in completing assignments you were given responsibility for. Graduation is a statement of faithfulness to your assignment. If you are unfaithful you are made to repeat or expelled. The faithful are promoted in life, the unfaithful are demoted, fired and end up in prison. If you work in a bank and you are unfaithful in watching the money you were entrusted with, your job is taken away and you could end up in prison. Learn to be faithful.

Lesson #36 - Leaders Know How to Conduct Themselves

One of the issues that many leaders face is "how to act". There is a level of responsibility that goes along with leadership and leaders should know how to conduct themselves in a manner that is in keeping with their position. If a leader does not conduct himself in the right way, followers have no incentive to adhere to a standard that their leader or leaders do not keep. If we look at the example of a parent, it is difficult for a parent to tell his child not to use drugs or engage in violence if the parent is abusing drugs and acting in a violent manner. Leaders are supposed to uphold the standard that they ask others to follow. As a future leader you must learn at an early age what is good and right conduct and what is wrong conduct. I saw a story recently about the mayor of a famous city. He held the high position of mayor but he was getting drunk publicly, using cocaine and cavorting with prostitutes. His conduct was not in keeping with his position. How can he enforce laws that he himself is breaking? How could he hold others accountable when he himself is not accountable? Leaders ensure that they behave in a certain manner especially if they are exposed to the public. Good leaders learn what conduct is appropriate for their position and ensure that their behaviour is exemplary. A young leader in the Bible was given this admonition, "1Ti. 4:12 Don't let anyone look down on you because you are young, but set an example for the believers in speech, in life, in love, in faith and in purity."

Lesson #37 – Leaders Practice for Their Moment

Leaders do not wait for the moment to arrive to prepare, they prepare in anticipation of the moments arrival. Followers often wait for things to come to them or begin preparing when they see a special moment coming. Leaders are prepared well before their big moment arrives. They have already envisioned their moment's arrival and have rehearsed what they will do at the appointed time. A great leader has their acceptance speech prepared long before they receive their award. As I grew as a leader I began to anticipate that I would be invited to speak at places that I never thought about before. I prepared my speeches and teachings and rehearsed what I would say if was invited long before I was invited. When the invitation came I was already there before in my mind.

In sports the term 'lucky shot' is often used to describe a shot made by a player. In most cases the shot may appear to be lucky but in reality instead of luck it was preparation meeting opportunity. I recall a conversation on ESPN about Ray Allen considered one of the greatest if not the greatest three point shooter of all time. He had hit a last second shot that essentially saved the season for the Miami Heat and allowed them to win back to back NBA championships. One pundit exclaimed that the Miami Heat won the game because of a lucky shot. Ray Allen then explained that for years he would enter the gym, cut off the lights and have someone turn on the lights and he would run to a spot on the court and have his assistant throw him the ball and he would envision only one second to shoot and he would launch the shot. He would do this over and over again envisioning a crowd of hostile fans and the opposing team charging at him. He did it so often that when the moment came he had already been there. What seemed like a lucky shot was in reality a well-rehearsed and calculated attempt that he knew he could make. Leaders live like this they are prepared for the moment. 2Ti. 4:2 "Preach the Word; be prepared in season and out of season; correct, rebuke and encourage — with great patience and careful instruction."

Lesson # 38 – Leaders are Examples

Followers have a lower level of accountability than leaders. If no one is following you what you do does not have the same consequence as when you are a leader. Followers look to leaders to see what they should do. If you desire to be a leader you have to prepare to be an example. Your life should be a testimony of what you speak about and you should be the example of what you speak about. This scriptural reference in 1Ti. 4:12 explains this thought well, "Don't let anyone look down on you because you are young, but set an example for the believers in speech, in life, in love, in faith and in purity". The apostle Paul who was the mentor was explaining to his mentee Timothy the requirements of a leader. He was saying be an example to your peers so that what you speak about is validated. He also told Timothy and others, "follow me as I follow Christ". My children do not have to look to others to figure out what a father should be like, I am the example. They do not have to search for the example of a mother; their mother is the resident example. It is better to have others follow what you do rather than what you say.

Lesson #39 – Leaders Have Personal Character

The road to success begins with Character. Talent is a great asset in life but talent will not sustain you. Talent can take you to the top but character will keep you there. Character is "Moral excellence, distinctive qualities, a good name, a good reputation". Character is what you do when no one is looking. There have been many athletes, politicians, preachers and persons of influence who have reached lofty heights only to lose it all because of a lack of character. They cheated on their spouse, stole or did something when they assumed no one was watching. Remember this, talent will take you a lot of places, but it is character that will keep you there. Never underestimate the value of Character. When employers are looking for workers they prefer persons of character who they can trust. Employers do background checks because they want to ascertain the character of a worker before they entrust them with their resources. In politics, religion and business we see many examples of persons who lost their office, lost their churches or business because of a lack of character. Your character is often your most valuable asset next to your God given gift or talent and should be viewed in light of its importance.

Lesson #40 – Leaders Understand the Power of Ideas

The most valuable commodity in the world is not gold, currency or diamonds. If we look at the most successful people in the world they often did not start out with much money. What distinguished them and cause their ascendance was an idea. Steve Jobs of Apple Computers had no money as an 18 year old but he had an idea. Mark Zuckerberg the creator of Facebook was a college student with limited wealth but he ended up as a multi billionaire because of an idea. Bill Gates the founder of Microsoft was also a college drop out with little resources yet he ended up as the richest man in the world simply because he kept thinking. Leaders are thinkers, they constantly spend time searching for ideas that will make their lives and the lives of others better or solve a problem. Whenever you come up with an idea that solves a human problem you are on your way to wealth because money follows good ideas. Bored people usually have no ideas. It is almost impossible for a leader to be bored because the world has so many problems and there are so many opportunities out there. Leaders consume information to acquire knowledge which is then translated into ideas that change the world. Leaders are readers, leaders are consumers of information, and leaders are thinkers. Leaders are possibility thinkers. Leaders are constantly searching to answer the question, "is it possible!"

Lesson #41 – Leaders Understand and Submit to Authority

Every leader begins as a follower. Every parent with the exception of Adam and Eve began as a child. Before you become a parent you must learn how to be a child which means you must submit to your parents so you can learn the lessons necessary for a successful life. In the same way a future leader has to learn to submit to the current leaders so that they can learn the lessons that will translate to their future ascent into leadership. The Bible states in Hebrews 13:17 "Obey your leaders and submit to their authority. They keep watch over you as men who must give an account. Obey them so that their work will be a joy, not a burden, for that would be of no advantage to you". In other words submission puts you in a position to be protected while you learn the principles needed for you to become an effective leader.

Lesson #42 – Leaders are Make Decisions and Take Initiative

A leader learns to make decisions without awaiting the approval of friends. A leader sets goals and decides to pursue them regardless of what others think. A leader "makes up his mind!" Good leaders are decisive and not afraid to make a wrong decision. If you are afraid of making a wrong decision you may never make a decision because every decision is potentially a wrong decision. A good leader searches and evaluates and after reviewing the facts makes the best decision with the information he has. Sometimes your decisions will be correct, other times they will not be correct. Your consciences should be clear when you make a decision. If your decision turns out to be wrong you will have an opportunity to correct and adjust. A good leader learns that over time they will make more right decisions than wrong and they therefore become confident as a decision maker.

Leaders take initiative while followers wait for someone to take the initiative or solve the problem. A leader is not afraid of taking responsibility or being exposed to risk. A leader will direct action with the understanding that action is required to prevent adversity, maintain stability or solve a problem.

Lesson #43 - Leaders Use Technology and Media

Leaders understand the value of tools. Tools are used to assist in making your work easier whatever the work is. In times past, if you needed to chop wood, the appropriate tool used to be the axe which allowed you to chop more efficiently. As technology evolved an electronic chain saw did the same job in a fraction of the time. In a similar way a written and post mailed letter was the most effective communication tool for worldwide communication for many years. The letter has been replaced by email so what would have taken weeks now takes seconds. A good leader learns to master and use the tools that advance their lives and purpose. Leaders take advantage of technology because technology allows them to do things in a quicker and more efficient manner. Technology is constantly changing but a leader will review current technologies and determine what is most appropriate to advance their cause. I have learned to take advantage of technology. I use computers, laptops, tablets, e-mail, cell phones, smartphones, Facebook, twitter, Instagram and anything else that puts me in a position to influence others positively. Technology can be used or abused. Abused means abnormally used. Leaders use media for good whether it is television, radio, internet, podcast, video, audio or whatever else is available.

Lesson #44 - Leaders Are Self- Driven

One of the most distinguishing factors that differentiate followers and ordinary people from leaders is that Leaders are self-driven. Leaders do not need an alarm clock to wake up in the morning. Leaders are so excited about each new day and looking forward to what they will accomplish that a clock is not necessary, they can't wait to get up and change the world. Leaders never feel like they have enough day to work with so they are anxious to get started and maximize the opportunities available. Leaders do not wait for ideas or solutions, they are constantly thinking on their own without external prodding. Followers often need others to motivate them and help them get started but leaders need no such motivation, they are internally motivated. Leaders are never finished because as soon as one problem is solved or one mission accomplished they are already on to the next phases. Followers try to make it through another day; leaders are ready to make the next day happen. My life has been filled with excitement, challenge, opportunity, struggle and victory because I drive myself. If your parents, teachers, friends or others have to constantly encourage you to do something you know you are not a leader yet.

Lesson #45 – Leaders have a Leadership Diet

You are the product of what you ingest, physically, mentally and spiritually. What do you watch, listen to and read? What do you eat physically? If you want changes in your health the doctor will advise you to change your diet to preserve your life. The same thing applies to your mental and spiritual diet. If you want improved mental and spiritual health you have to change what you watch and listen to. What you watch and listen to influences your thoughts which then influences your philosophy which determines you actions and lifestyle. A good leader can't afford to waste time on unproductive thinking so the good leader will ingest only things mentally, spiritually and physically that increases their value, preserves their life and advances their cause. As a young adult I began a journey that changed my life. I first changed my mental state by determining that I would only watch and listen to what had a positive impact on my life. I eliminated many things I used to watch. It was only later in my life that I realized that I also needed to change my physical diet. Because I was an athlete and felt healthy for years I did not care what I ate. Later in life my diet had a negative on my body and I began to attract illnesses. Because of my condition I sought out information and learned which foods benefitted my body and changed my diet. When I changed my diet my body improved. If you change your physical diet if you can change your shape. If you change your mental diet you can change your mind and shape a better future. Leaders ingest what improves their being and value. Develop a leadership diet.

Leadership Lesson #46 – Leaders Understand Order

When you represent the King you understand how he set things up, his order. God – Parents – Children – TEACHER – STUDENT. True leaders understand order and have relationships in order.

Never allow the disorder around you to reorder your world. A true leader does not try to usurp authority or disrespect the persons naturally above them in the chain of order. Persons who try to usurp authority often end up incarcerated because violations of natural order results in chaos, disorder or anarchy. Usurpers are punished externally because they refuse to take internal control.

A young leader is a leader who respects and learns life lessons from parents – teachers, adult leaders, the law and legal system and each other. Righteous young leaders have appropriate respect according to God's order. Disrespect breeds disrespect.

Protocol is not a bad word to a leader because they understand that true leaders will flourish within established protocol and end up at the top by respecting others and learning from them and putting into practice the things they have learned when they rise in the chain of order.

Lesson #47 - Leaders Are Loyal

One of the distinguishing characteristics of a leader is loyalty. When a leader has benefitted from a mentor or anyone who has influenced their growth or success they maintain an intense loyalty. Leaders are loyal to friends, leaders, parents and others in face of criticism and misunderstanding because they value others who have contributed to their lives. Leaders realize that everyone including themselves have faults and shortcomings and they are not easily swayed to become disloyal when other criticize their friends, leaders or mentors by pointing out faults. Leaders focus on the good contributions of others and remember those who have helped them get to where they are. A leader does not ignore wrong or fail to address it but never abandons friends, mentors, parents or leaders who have helped them. Loyalty does not mean blindness or ignoring criminal activity. We are not required to be loyal to despots. We are required to be loyal under the normal rules of life, family, politics, business or spiritual life.

Lesson #48 – Leaders Understand Forgiveness

The greatest teacher that ever lived noted that you must forgive if you want to be forgiven. True leaders are people of forgiveness. Great leaders are known for their ability to forgive those who have done the cruelest things to them. Dr. Martin Luther King, Nelson Mandela and Mahatma Gandhi are prime examples of persons who had a reason to harbor hate and unforgiveness. Yet they forgave and used forgiveness to propel them to personal and national success. A leader understands that forgiveness can overcome hate and prejudice and produce reconciliation while transforming the lives of both the forgiver and the forgiven. Nelson Mandela put it this way, "When you harbor unforgiveness and hatred it is like drinking poison and hoping your enemy will die". This is a powerful statement that demonstrate the negative power of hatred and unforgiveness. Great leaders realize that we have all benefitted from forgiveness so we must forgive. God forgave us, our parents have forgiven us at some point and others have forgiven us for wrong we have done so we must learn to forgive. A part of the Lord's Prayer indicates, "Forgive us our debt as we forgive our debtors."

Lesson #49 – Leaders have Compassion

The greatest leaders are recognized for their compassion. They are motivated to alleviate suffering and to bring hope and comfort to the downtrodden. Leaders have a difficult time walking away from persons who are suffering. The Bible speaks of Jesus being "moved" with compassion. Compassion causes a leader to act on behalf of those he or she sees are disadvantaged or vulnerable. One of the great examples of compassion was the nun known as "Mother Theresa". She had compassion on the diseased and downtrodden in India and did all she could to help those who were suffering. A great leader cannot ignore suffering and distress. A great leader will have compassion and be compelled to act to assist those who are suffering. Leaders who lack compassion tend to take advantage of the poor and needy and step on them when they are down. They are often selfish and inwardly focused. A great leader not only focuses his or her circle of friends and family and on themselves but also focuses on the people who have needs in their communities.

Lesson #50 - Leaders Are Great Communicators

It is hard to be a great leader without being able to communicate your ideas in a manner that motivates others to action. One does not necessarily have to be a great orator or speaker but if you are unable to communicate effectively it is difficult to spur others into action. The great leader will cause others to follow because they are attracted to the ideas, plans and visions that the leader communicates through word, action and influence. It certainly helps to be a great speaker but speaking is not the only form of communication. A leader learns to communicate by putting things on paper in a coherent manner that others can come behind and receive direction from. A great leader learns to write the vision down and make it plain.

Leadership Scriptures

2Ti. 4:2,5 - [2] Preach the Word; be prepared in season and out of season; correct, rebuke and encourage — with great patience and careful instruction. [5] But you, keep your head in all situations, endure hardship, do the work of an evangelist, discharge all the duties of your ministry.

Mt. 15:14 - Leave them; they are blind guides. [Some manuscripts: guides of the blind] If a blind man leads a blind man, both will fall not a pit."

Mt. 18:1-2,4 - [1] At that time the disciples came to Jesus and asked, "Who is the greatest in the kingdom of heaven?" [2] He called a little child and had him stand among them. And he said: "I tell you the truth, unless you change and become like little children, you will never enter the kingdom of heaven. [4] Therefore, whoever humbles himself like this child is the greatest in the kingdom of heaven.

1Ti. 4:12,14-16 - [12] Don't let anyone look down on you because you are young, but set an example for the believers in speech, in life, in love, in faith and in purity. [14] Do not neglect the gift that is in you, which was given to you by prophecy with the laying on of the hands of the eldership. [15] Be diligent in these matters; give yourself wholly to them, so that everyone may see your progress. [16] Watch your life and doctrine closely. Persevere in them, because if you do, you will save both yourself and your hearers.

Mt. 20:26-28 - [26] Not so with you. Instead, whoever wants to become great among you must be your servant, [27] and whoever wants to be first must be your slave [28] just as the Son of Man did not come to be served, but to serve, and to give his life as a ransom for many.

Tit. 2:6 - Similarly, encourage the young men to be self-controlled. In everything set them an example by doing what is good. In your teaching show integrity, seriousness and soundness of speech that cannot be condemned, so that those who oppose you may be ashamed because they have nothing bad to say about us.

Isaiah 60:1-3 - New King James Version (NKJV) -
[1] Arise, shine;
For your light has come!
And the glory of the Lord is risen upon you.
[2] For behold, the darkness shall cover the earth,
And deep darkness the people;
But the Lord will arise over you,
And His glory will be seen upon you.
[3] The Gentiles shall come to your light,
And kings to the brightness of your rising.

Matt 5:13-16 - "You are the salt of the earth; but if the salt loses its flavor, how shall it be seasoned? It is then good for nothing but to be thrown out and trampled underfoot by men.
[14] "You are the light of the world. A city that is set on a hill cannot be hidden. [15] Nor do they light a lamp and put it under a basket, but on a lampstand, and it gives light to all who are in the house. [16] Let your light so shine before men, that they may see your good works and glorify your Father in heaven.

Eph 5:15-18 - [15] See then that you walk circumspectly, not as fools but as wise, [16] redeeming the time, because the days are evil. [17] Therefore do not be unwise, but understand what the will of the Lord is. [18] And do not be drunk with wine (lower value), in which is dissipation; but be filled with the Spirit (higher value).

Philippians 12 - [12] Not that I have already attained, or am already perfected; but I press on, that I may lay hold of that for which Christ Jesus has also laid hold of me. [13] Brethren, I do not count myself to have apprehended; but one thing I do, forgetting those things which are behind and reaching forward to those things which are ahead, [14] I press toward the goal for the prize of the upward call of God in Christ Jesus.

2 Timothy 2:1-4 - [1] You therefore, my son, be strong in the grace that is in Christ Jesus. [2] And the things that you have heard from me among many witnesses, commit these to faithful men who will be able to teach others also. [3] You therefore must endure[a] hardship as a good soldier of Jesus Christ. [4]No one engaged in warfare entangles himself with the affairs of this life, that he may please him who enlisted him as a soldier.

I Tim 3:1-5- [1] This is a faithful saying: If a man desires the position of a bishop,[a] he desires a good work. [2] A bishop then must be blameless, the husband of one wife, temperate, sober-minded, of good behavior, hospitable, able to teach; 3 not given to wine, not violent, not greedy for money,[b] but gentle, not quarrelsome, not covetous; with all longsuffering and teaching. [3] For the time will come when they will not endure sound doctrine, but according to their own desires, because they have itching ears, they will heap up for themselves teachers; [4] and they will turn their ears away from the truth, and be turned aside to fables. [5] But you be watchful in all things, endure afflictions, do the work of an evangelist, fulfill your ministry.

Joshua 1:8 (New International Version)
Do not let this Book of the Law depart from your mouth; meditate on it day and night, so that you may be careful to

do everything written in it. Then you will be prosperous and successful.

Pr. 31:2 - “O my son, O son of my womb, O son of my vows do not spend your strength on women, your vigor on those who ruin kings. “It is not for kings, O Lemuel — not for kings to drink wine, not for rulers to crave beer, lest they drink and forget what the law decrees, and deprive all the oppressed of their rights. Give beer to those who are perishing, wine to those who are in anguish; let them drink and forget their poverty and remember their misery no more.

Psalm 119 - 9 How can a young man keep his way pure? By living according to your word. 10 I seek you with all my heart; do not let me stray from your commands. 11 I have hidden your word in my heart that I might not sin against you. 12 Praise be to you, O LORD; teach me your decrees. 13 With my lips I recount all your laws.

Titus 2 1:6 - Likewise, exhort the young men to be sober-minded, 7 in all things showing yourself to be a pattern of good works; in doctrine showing integrity, reverence, incorruptibility,[a] 8 sound speech that cannot be condemned, that one who is an opponent may be ashamed, having nothing evil to say of you.

DR. DAVID BURROWS & RAYMOND ENEAS
THE GOOD SUCCESS TOUR
IF YOU WANT TO LEARN HOW TO:
• Be successful based on God's standards
• Develop personal success in life
• Position yourself for greater success
• Learn & harness the principles of success
• Experience success in your relationships
• Become successful in business
• Help others to become successful
DAVE BURROWS
Real Success
THE LAWS OF GOOD SUCCESS
Mastering the keys of success
FOREWORD BY DR MYLES MUNROE
RAYMOND ENEAS
THE MIND OF SUCCESS
THEN CONTACT US TO DO A GOOD SUCCESS EVENT AT YOUR CHURCH OR ORGANIZATION.
PH: 954-603-7285 OR 407-777-8872 / www.daveburrowsministries.com

Booking Form

Church/Organization & Contact Person *

City, State , Zip Code *

Phone & Email *

Dates Requested *

Type of Event & Theme *

Target & Expected Audience *

Honorarium Amount *

Will host ministry cover travel and accomodations for spouse or road assistant *

How did you hear about Dave Burrows Ministries *

PROVEN
Transformational
STRATEGIES
for Reaching & Impacting
Teens, Parents
& Families
YOUTH AND FAMILY
SPECIALIST
DR. DAVE BURROWS
For booking
Call Us at 954-603-7285
pastordaveburrows@hotmail.com
www.daveburrowsministries.com
Follow Us
24 HOUR NETWORK | VIDEO ON DEMAND | LIVE BROADCAST
WATCH OUR 24 HOUR NETWORK OR VIDEO ON DEMAND PROGRAMS
POWERED BY
LifeStream.tv

Dave Burrows Resource Products
Books, CD's & DVD's | 954-603-7285
www. bfmmm.com | www.daveburrowsministries.com
DAVE BURROWS MINISTRIES
YOUTH & FAMILY
SPECIALIST
DAVE BURROWS
STARTING A BUSINESS
MAXIMIZING TECHNOLOGY
MYLES MUNROE
& DAVID BURROWS
KINGDOM PARENTING
THE RUFFNECK PASTOR
DVD
Sex & Dating
A Guide to Relationships for Teens and Young Adults
DAVE BURROWS
DAVE BURROWS
YOUTH MINISTRY TRAINING COURSE
REVELATIONS FROM The Life & Testimony of Pastor Dave "Davy B" Burrows
WANTED
Madison County
David M. Burrows
THE POWER OF
POSITIVE CHOICES
PASTOR DAVE BURROWS
Foreword by Dr. Myles Munroe and Robyn Gool
Talk to Me
A Guide for dialogue between Parents and Teens.
THE RUFFNECK PASTOR
DAVE BURROWS
Strategies for saving the next generation
Dave Burrows
THE RUFFNECK PASTOR
Keys TO BECOMING A Great FATHER
PASTOR DAVE BURROWS
FAMILY SPECIALIST
WinnersTouch
DAVE M. BURROWS
BUSINESS CONSULTANT • MOTIVATIONAL SPEAKER
• COMPUTER TECHNOLOGY CONSULTANT
Who or What is a Winner?
Winning with Teamwork
DVD